The Ultimate Cheese Balls Cookbook

25 Amazing Cheese Balls Recipes

BY: SOPHIA FREEMAN

COPYRIGHTED

Liability

This publication is meant as an informational tool. The individual purchaser accepts all liability if damages occur because of following the directions or guidelines set out in this publication. The Author bears no responsibility for reparations caused by the misuse or misinterpretation of the content.

Copyright

* * * ★ ★ ★ ★ ★ ★ ★ * * *

My gift to you!

Thank you, cherished reader, for purchasing my book and taking the time to read it. As a special reward for your decision, I would like to offer a gift of free and discounted books directly to your inbox. All you need to do is fill in the box below with your email address and name to start getting amazing offers in the comfort of your own home. You will never miss an offer because a reminder will be sent to you. Never miss a deal and get great deals without having to leave the house! Subscribe now and start saving!

Subscribe to the Newsletter!

Your email address   Subscribe

Table of Contents

Chapter I - Cheese Balls with Sausages, Parmesan Cheese, Cheddar Cheese and Arancinis

zzzzzzzzzzzzzzzzzzzzzzzzzzzzzzzzzzzzzzzzzzzzzzzzzzzzz

1) Cheese and Potato Cheese Balls

These cheese balls are made with potato filling which give them a soft and gooey texture. Crispy on the outside and the filling of potato inside this cheese ball is a must try for everyone out there.

Total Prep Time: 30 minutes

Makes: 16

Ingredient List:

- Potatoes peeled: 2
- Egg yolks: 6
- Melted butter: ¼ cup
- White pepper: as per taste
- Salt: as per taste
- Shredded cheddar cheese: 2 cups
- Onion, cubed: ½
- Eggs: 2
- Water: ¼ cup
- Flour: 1 cup
- Bread crumbs: 1 cup
- Oil to fry

zzzzzzzzzzzzzzzzzzzzzzzzzzzzzzzzzzzzzzzzzzzzzzzzzzzzzzzzzz

Instructions:

Boil all potatoes in salted water until tender. Peel and mash potatoes and keep them aside.

Once the potato turns cool, stir in melted butter, salt, and white pepper. Now add the egg yolks and cheddar cheese in potatoes. Now add the chopped onions in potatoes. Make round balls with this mixture and place them in the fridge for about half an hour.

Dip:

Make a dip by mixing eggs and water in a bowl. Dip the balls one by one in this dip and then coat with the bread crumbs. Fry all potato balls in preheated oil in a wok until they turn golden brown. Serve hot.

2) Yummy Cheese Ball

This recipe is of a nice and yummy cheese ball with a filling of your own choice of meat and lots of cheese. They are best served with butter crackers.

Total Prep Time: four hours

Makes: 20

Ingredient List:

- Bacon: 1 pound
- Cream cheese: 16 ounces
- Mayonnaise: 3 Tbsp.
- Green onion chopped: 1 bunch
- Chopped pecans: 1 cup

zzzzzzzzzzzzzzzzzzzzzzzzzzzzzzzzzzzzzzzzzzzzzzzzzzzz

Instructions:

Fry all bacon strips on a hot skillet. Combine the bacon and cream cheese in one bowl. Mix the mayonnaise and the green onion in bacon mixture. Mix all ingredients well and make small balls from the mixture. Coat each ball with the chopped pecans and refrigerate for a few hours before serving them.

3) Buffalo Chicken Cheese Balls

This cheese ball has a very hot and spicy flavor and can be served with a nice dip to go with it. The pepper jack cheese adds to the amazing flavor of the cheese ball. Following is the recipe of it.

Total Prep Time: 2 hours 15 minutes

Makes: 12

Ingredient List:

- Chicken breast: 1 pound
- Green onions chopped: ½ cup
- Shredded cheddar cheese: 1 cup
- Shredded pepper jack cheese: 1 cup
- Hot pepper sauce: 1 cup
- Ranch dressing: ½ cup
- Flour: 1 cup
- Eggs: 3
- Bread crumbs: 1 ½ cup

zzzzzzzzzzzzzzzzzzzzzzzzzzzzzzzzzzzzzzzzzzzzzzzzzzzzz

Instructions:

Mix the chicken breast, green onions, cheddar cheese, pepper jack cheese, ranch dressing, and hot pepper sauce in one bowl. Mix all the ingredients and make small balls from this mixture. Coat all balls in flour and then dip each ball into beaten eggs.

Finally coat all balls in the bread crumbs. Heat oil and fry all balls until they turn golden brown. Serve hot with your favorite sauce.

4) Sausage Cheese Balls

These cheese balls are made out of either chicken sausages or pork sausages. They are very delicious in taste and are mostly used in Christmas parties.

Total Prep Time: 20 minutes

Makes: 24

Ingredient List:

- Pork or chicken sausage: 1 pound
- Butter milk: 1 ½ cup
- Shredded cheddar cheese: 4 cups
- Chopped onion: ½
- Garlic powder: ½ tsp.

zzzzzzzzzzzzzzzzzzzzzzzzzzzzzzzzzzzzzzzzzzzzzzzzzzzzz

Instructions:

You can bake or fry cheese balls as per your taste.

Mix the sausages, butter milk, cheddar cheese, green onion and the celery in one bowl. Season this mixture with the garlic powder. Make as many balls as you can, and bake at 375 degrees Fahrenheit or deep fry them.

5) Fried Macaroni And Cheese Balls

These fried mac and cheese balls are an absolute favorite of everyone, especially kids. They are super cheesy to eat. It's like one can't stop having them. They are simply never enough!

Total Prep Time: 40 minutes

Makes: 8

Ingredient List:

- Macaroni & cheese mix: 7.25 ounces
- Butter: 2 Tbsp.
- Milk: ¼ cup
- Paprika: ½ tsp.
- Shredded cheddar cheese: 1 cup
- Italian Bread crumbs: 2 cups
- Italian cheese blend: 1 cup
- Pimento cheese spread: ¾ cup
- Chili powder: ½ tsp.
- Black pepper: ½ tsp.
- Sugar: ½ tsp.
- Salt: ¼ tsp.
- Eggs: 4
- Milk: 3 Tbsp.
- Peanut oil for frying

zzzzzzzzzzzzzzzzzzzzzzzzzzzzzzzzzzzzzzzzzzzzzzzzzzzzzz

Instructions:

Fill one pot with salted water and let it rolling boil over high flame. Mix in macaroni and let it boil again. Cook well without covering for almost 7 minutes. Drain macaroni and mix in butter (2 Tbsp.), milk (¼ cup) and cheese from packet.

Mix in the cheddar cheese, Italian cheese blend and the pimento cheese spread in hot mixture. Mix well and put in refrigerator for almost 4 hours.

Line one baking dish with parchment paper. Make balls with this mixture and put on parchment paper and refrigerate for 2 hours to make balls firm.

Beat remaining milk and eggs. Add salt, sugar, black pepper, chili powder, and paprika into bread crumbs. Dip the balls first in the egg mixture and then coat in the bread crumb mixture and fry in oil to make them golden brown. Serve hot.

6) Arancini Cheese Balls

These cheese balls are made with an Italian rice ball made in white wine risotto and a filling of mozzarella cheese. These cheese balls can be frozen also so it is a great idea to store them in the freezer and take out when unexpected guests arrive suddenly.

Total Prep Time: 20 minutes

Makes: 18

Ingredient List:

- Chopped onion: 1
- Olive oil: 1 Tbsp.
- Salt: as per taste
- Black pepper: as per taste
- Chopped ham: 2 ounces
- White wine: ½ cup
- Uncooked Arborio rice: 1 cup
- Crushed garlic: 1 clove
- Parmesan cheese: ½ cup
- Egg: 1
- Milk: 1 Tbsp.
- Dry bread crumbs: 2 cups
- Flour: ½ cup
- Mozzarella cheese: 5 ounces
- Oil for frying
- Chicken stock: 2 ½ cups
- Peas: ½ cup

zzzzzzzzzzzzzzzzzzzzzzzzzzzzzzzzzzzzzzzzzzzzzzzzzzzzz

Instructions:

Take a saucepan and add in the olive oil. Fry the onion until transparent and stir in garlic. Now add the Arborio rice and white wine in a saucepan. Stir well and pour in the chicken stock. Once the rice is cooked and the liquid evaporated, add in the peas and ham. Now season this mixture with salt and pepper. Mix the parmesan cheese in a saucepan and remove it from heat. Let the mixture cool.

Now add one egg in the mixture. Take another bowl and mix egg and the milk together in this bowl. Make balls with the mixture and make an indent in the middle of cheese ball, put one mozzarella cheese cube in the indent and enclose this cheese by giving it the shape of a ball. Replicate this procedure with remaining balls. Dip each ball into the flour then milk and egg mixture, and finally coat in the bread crumbs.

Heat oil in a large wok and fry all cheese balls in small batches until they turn golden brown. Serve hot with your favorite sauce.

7) Italian Cheese Balls

This cheese ball is a mixture of the pecans, tomato sauce and the spice known as cumin. It is a bit different from the other cheese balls as its ingredients are a bit different. These cheese balls can also be stored in the freezer for future use.

Total Prep Time: one hour

Makes: 6

Ingredient List:

- Pecans: 1 cup
- Bread crumbs: 1 cup
- Shredded cheddar cheese: ½ cup
- Egg: 1
- Chopped onion: 1
- Vegetable oil: 2 cups
- Tomato juice: 1 cup
- Condensed Tomato soup: 10.75 ounces
- Ground cumin: 1 tsp.

zzzzzzzzzzzzzzzzzzzzzzzzzzzzzzzzzzzzzzzzzzzzzzzzzzzzzzz

Instructions:

In a bowl, mix in the pecans, bread crumbs, cheddar cheese, egg and the chopped onion. Mix properly and form balls from the mixture. Refrigerate them for half an hour.

Bake the cheese balls in the oven at 175 degree Fahrenheit.

For the sauce: Mix the tomato soup, tomato juice and the grounded cumin in one bowl. Drizzle this sauce on the balls before serving them.

8) Cheesy Chicken Balls

These cheese balls are made with chicken with a filling of both mozzarella and cheddar cheese with a bit of seasoning variety. They are very delicious in taste.

Total Prep Time: 30 minutes

Makes: 18

Ingredient List:

- Chicken mince: ½ kg
- Salt: as per taste
- White pepper: as per taste
- 8 to 10 grinded green chilies
- 2 eggs
- Cubed mozzarella cheese: 5 ounces
- Shredded cheddar cheese: 1 ¾ cup
- Bread crumbs: 2 cups
- Oil: for frying

zzzzzzzzzzzzzzzzzzzzzzzzzzzzzzzzzzzzzzzzzzzzzzzzzzzzzzzzz

Instructions:

Mix the chicken mince, salt, pepper, grinded green chilies, one egg and the shredded cheddar cheese in one bowl. Mix all the ingredients properly. Now form balls and in each ball, make an indent with your thumb. Put one little cube of the mozzarella cheese in this indent and enclose the ball to completely cover the cheese cube in the ball. Coat the balls in egg, and dry bread crumbs. Fry them in hot oil and serve with your favorite sauce.

9) Bacon-Bleu Cheese Ball

This recipe includes both the blue cheese and the cream cheese. It is extremely cheesy to eat and the cheese literally oozes out when you bite in to the cheese ball.

Total Prep Time: 3 hours

Makes: 20

Ingredient List:

- Cream cheese: 16 ounces
- Bacon or chicken: 3 ounces.
- Blue cheese crumbled: 3 ounces
- Blue cheese salad dressing: ¼ cup
- Green onions chopped: one bunch
- Garlic powder: ½ tsp.
- Dried parsley: 1 cup

zzzzzzzzzzzzzzzzzzzzzzzzzzzzzzzzzzzzzzzzzzzzzzzzzzzz

Instructions:

In a bowl, mix cream cheese and the blue cheese. It is time to mix meat in cheese mixture. Stir in the salad dressing and season with the garlic powder. Add in the green onions and mix properly. Make balls from the mixture. Refrigerate for few hours and coat with dried parsley before serving.

10) Spinach Arancini

This is another version of the Italian cheese balls, this time not only with rice but also with a filling of spinach which has a great healthy value and nutritional value as well.

Total Prep Time: 1 hour 30 minutes

Makes: 24

Ingredient List:

- Olive oil: 2 Tbsp.
- Chopped onion: 1
- Chopped garlic: 2 cloves chopped
- Arborio rice: ¾ cup
- White wine: ½ cup
- Spinach leaves: 1 cup
- Chicken broth: 2 cups
- Oil to fry
- Butter: 1 Tbsp.
- Mozzarella cheese cubed: 1 ½ cups
- Flour: ½ cup
- Water: 1 Tbsp.
- Bread crumbs: 1 ½ cups
- Egg: 1

ZZZZZZZZZZZZZZZZZZZZZZZZZZZZZZZZZZZZZZZZZZZZZZZZZZZZZZZ

Instructions:

In olive oil, sauté onion and garlic, and then add in the Arborio rice, white wine, chicken broth and cook well, until the rice have been cooked. Add the pepper and salt to taste and now add the spinach and mix well. Put this mixture in the fridge.

Make balls from this mixture and make an indent with your thumb to add cube of the mozzarella cheese. Mix egg and water in a bowl and coat these balls into this mixture and then coat with bread crumbs. Frying them until they turn golden brown.

Chapter II - Spicy Cheese Ball, Spinach, Mango Cheese Balls and Pineapple One

zzzzzzzzzzzzzzzzzzzzzzzzzzzzzzzzzzzzzzzzzzzzzzzzzzzz

11) Easy Beef Cheese Balls

These cheese balls are very easy to make and are perfect for every kind of occasion and event. They can be made in to any kind of shape for instance, ball shape, log shape, snowman etc.

Total Prep Time: 30 minutes

Makes: 15

Ingredient List:

- Cream cheese: 24 ounces
- Green onion, chopped: 1 bunch
- Dry and chopped beef: 8 ounces
- Chopped pecans: 1 cup

zzzzzzzzzzzzzzzzzzzzzzzzzzzzzzzzzzzzzzzzzzzzzzzzzzzzz

Instructions:

In a mixing bowl, add in the cooked beef, the chopped green onions, and the cream cheese. Mix all the ingredients properly and make round balls and coat each ball with the chopped pecans. Place the balls in a tray, cover them with plastic wrap and refrigerate for few hours before serving.

12) Mango Chutney Cheese Ball

These cheese balls have a very yummy and cheesy flavor along with mango chutney flavor. They are very simple to make and have amazing taste.

Total Prep Time: Almost 3 hours.

Makes: 6

Ingredient List:

- 1 cup of raisins
- 11 ounces of cream cheese
- 2 ounces Cooked chicken or bacon
- 1 bunch Green onions, chopped
- 3 Tbsp. sour cream
- Mango chutney: To Serve

zzzzzzzzzzzzzzzzzzzzzzzzzzzzzzzzzzzzzzzzzzzzzzzzzzzzzz

Instructions:

Take a bowl and mix in the cream cheese, raisins, sour cream, green onions, and cooked chicken or bacon. Mix all ingredients together and make round balls with this mixture. Put them in a tray and cover the balls with plastic wrap. Put in fridge for few hours. Before serving, drizzle with the mango chutney on top of the balls. The mango chutney gives the cheese balls a very unique and distinctive flavor.

13) Pineapple Cheese Balls

These cheese balls have a tingly flavor because of the pineapples. The pineapples give the cheese balls a very different and refreshing taste. They are absolutely mouthwatering.

Total Prep Time: 2 hours

Makes: 16

Ingredient List:

- Cream cheese: 16 ounces
- Celery: 1 cup
- Minced onion: 1 tsp.
- Drained and crushed Pineapple: 20 ounces
- Chopped pecans: 1 cup
- Chopped green bell pepper: 2

ZZZZZZZZZZZZZZZZZZZZZZZZZZZZZZZZZZZZZZZZZZZZZZZZZZZZZ

Instructions:

In a large bowl, combine the cream cheese, the chopped celery, the minced onion, pineapples, and the chopped green bell pepper in this bowl. Mix all the ingredients together and form round balls with this mixture. Coat each ball with chopped pecans and refrigerate them for a few hours before serving them.

14) Spicy Taco Cheese Balls

These cheese balls can be stored for a week, so it is a very handy recipe as one can prepare the cheese balls early ahead of their party. Its spicy taste really tingles the taste buds and they are best served with nachos.

Total Prep Time: 2 hours

Makes: 12

Ingredient List:

- Dried parsley: 1 Bunch
- Taco seasoning: 1.25 ounces
- Cream cheese: 8 ounces
- Shredded Mexican cheese blend: 4 cups
- Mayonnaise: ¼ cup
- Jalapeno pepper chopped, ¼ cup

zzzzzzzzzzzzzzzzzzzzzzzzzzzzzzzzzzzzzzzzzzzzzzzzzzzz

Instructions:

Take a bowl, put in the cream cheese, Mexican cheese blend, mayonnaise, jalapeno peppers and the taco seasoning and mix until everything is mixed and blended properly. Shape these into little balls and coat the balls with the chopped parsley to give green color to each ball.

Refrigerate them for few hours before serving preferably two hours or more. Make sure to coat them in a generous amount of parsley. It will give a great taste to your cheese balls.

15) Spinach Cheese Balls

This recipe of cheese balls can be really healthy especially for kids who try to avoid spinach and for elders also. It also has a good taste in fact the addition of spinach add to the flavor in these cheese balls.

Total Prep Time: 20 minutes

Makes: 8

Ingredient List:

- Chopped spinach: 10 ounces
- Cream cheese: 16 ounces
- Vegetable soup mix: 0.4 ounces
- Mayonnaise: 2 Tbsp.
- Cheddar cheese: 1 cup
- Chopped walnuts: ½ cup

zzzzzzzzzzzzzzzzzzzzzzzzzzzzzzzzzzzzzzzzzzzzzzzzzzzzzz

Instructions:

Take a bowl, add in the chopped spinach, cream cheese, vegetable soup mix, mayonnaise, cheddar cheese and mix all these ingredients. Make balls with this mixture and coat each ball with chopped walnuts. Put cheese balls in your fridge for a few hours before serving. You can serve them with crackers or a dip of your choice.

16) Easy Cheese Balls

These cheese balls are fairly very quick and easy to make. It is a very simple dish and can be a healthy snack for kids or for their lunch boxes. These can also be made when someone arrives unexpectedly at your house so you can make these and use as starters!

Total Prep Time: one hour

Makes: 10

Ingredient List:

- Cream cheese: 8 ounces
- Ranch dressing: 1 ounce
- Cheddar cheese: 2 ½ cups
- Chopped pecans: 1 ½ cups

ZZZZZZZZZZZZZZZZZZZZZZZZZZZZZZZZZZZZZZZZZZZZZZZZZZZZZZZZ

Instructions:

In a bowl, put the cream cheese, ranch dressing, and cheddar cheese in this bowl. Shape the mixture into little balls and coat each ball into chopped pecans. Make sure to completely coat all balls with pecans. Put the balls in the fridge for a few hours before serving them, preferably three hours or more.

Chapter III - Chocolate and Sweet Cheese Balls, Feta and Blue Cheese Combination with Cheese Balls

zzzzzzzzzzzzzzzzzzzzzzzzzzzzzzzzzzzzzzzzzzzzzzzzzzzzzz

17) Feta Cheese Balls

These cheese balls are very yummy and delicious in taste because of the flavor of garlic added. The minced garlic gives a different flavor. Feta cheese also gives a nice flavor.

Total Prep Time: 2 hours

Makes: 32

Ingredient List:

- Cream cheese: 16 ounces
- Feta cheese: 4 ounces
- Olive oil: 5 Tbsp.
- Chopped Green onions: 5
- Garlic cloves minced: 3
- Dried oregano: 2 tsp.
- Black pepper: 1 tsp.

zzzzzzzzzzzzzzzzzzzzzzzzzzzzzzzzzzzzzzzzzzzzzzzzzzzz

Instructions:

Take a bowl and add in the cream cheese, feta cheese and olive oil. Mix properly and season the cheese with the black pepper, garlic, dried oregano. Mix green onions in this mixture. Mix all the ingredients and form balls with this mixture. Refrigerate the balls overnight and serve with your favorite dip.

18) The Perfect Cheese Ball Recipe

This recipe of cheese ball is a must try for everyone because of the amazing ingredients it has. The taste of wine enhances the taste of the cheese ball and the cranberries added give a real twist to them. Further the taste of either the maple syrup or the pancake syrup will give a sweet taste to these cheese balls. Below is the recipe:

Total Prep Time: Almost 3 hours.

Makes: 6

Ingredient List:

- Cream cheese: 8 ounces
- Mozzarella cheese: 8 ounces
- Cranberries: ½ cup
- Wine: 2 Tbsp.
- Chopped pecans: ½ cup
- Maple or pancake syrup: ¼ cup

zzzzzzzzzzzzzzzzzzzzzzzzzzzzzzzzzzzzzzzzzzzzzzzzzzzzzzz

Instructions:

In a bowl, mix the cream cheese, mozzarella cheese and mix properly. Now stir in the wine and cranberries. Mix all the ingredients well. Now add in the pancake or the maple syrup.

Mix all things really well and make small balls with this mixture and coat all balls in chopped pecans. Put them in the fridge for few hours before serving them.

19) Chocolate Chip Cheese Balls

These cheese balls can be used for the purpose of desert as they are made out of the chocolate chips. The real chocolaty flavor gives a real boost to our taste buds and of course chocolates are everyone's favorites and can be a real treat to eat!

Total Prep Time: 3 hours

Makes: 20

Ingredient List:

- Cream cheese: 8 ounces
- Softened butter: ½ cup
- Vanilla extract: ¼ tsp.
- Brown sugar: Two Tbsp.
- Sugar: ¾ cup
- Semi-sweet chocolate chips: 1 cup
- Chopped pecans: ¾ cup

zzzzzzzzzzzzzzzzzzzzzzzzzzzzzzzzzzzzzzzzzzzzzzzzzzzzz

Instructions:

In a large bowl, mix in the cream cheese, vanilla extract, softened butter, granulated sugar and brown sugar. Mix all the ingredients well. Stir in the chocolate chips. Make small balls with this mixture and put all balls in a tray. Put in the fridge to chill for about two hours. Sprinkle chopped pecans on balls and serve chilled. You can also coat balls before putting in your fridge.

20) Bacon Ranch Cheese Balls

These cheese balls can be used as appetizers or a quick meal when a person is in a hurry because they are made out of bacon. You can even substitute the bacon with your own choice of meat, for instance chicken or even beef mince.

Total Prep Time: 15 minutes

Makes: 30

Ingredient List:

- Softened cream cheese: 16 ounces
- Bacon slices: 6
- Buttermilk and Ranch dressing mix: 1 ounce
- Cheddar cheese: ½ cup
- Chopped Green onions: 4
- Black olives, chopped: 3 Tbsp.
- Chopped pecans: 1 ½ cups

zzzzzzzzzzzzzzzzzzzzzzzzzzzzzzzzzzzzzzzzzzzzzzzzzzzz

Instructions:

Add the cream cheese and the bacon slices in a large bowl. Add in the ranch dressing mix, shredded cheddar cheese, olives and green onions. The olives and the green onions will give a unique flavor to cheese balls. Make ball shapes with this mixture and put in the fridge for a few hours. Coat each ball into chopped pecans before serving.

21) Blue Cheese Balls

Blue cheese is one of the most famous cheese in the world. It is known for its amazing and unique taste. You can use this blue cheese to make cheese balls out of it as well. Below is the recipe of it.

Total Prep Time: 20 minutes

Makes: 20

Ingredient List:

- Cream cheese: 16 ounces
- Shredded blue cheese: 1 cup
- Shredded cheddar cheese: 1 cup
- Minced onion: ¼ cup
- Worcestershire sauce: 1 Tbsp.
- Chopped walnuts: 1 cup

zzzzzzzzzzzzzzzzzzzzzzzzzzzzzzzzzzzzzzzzzzzzzzzzzzzzzz

Instructions:

In a bowl, combine cream cheese, blue cheese, cheddar cheese in this bowl. Add in the minced onion and Worcestershire sauce. Mix these ingredients well. Cover the bowl with plastic wrap and place in the fridge overnight. The next day, you can make small balls with this mixture and coat each ball with walnuts.

Chapter IV - Christmas Cheese Balls, Cheese Balls with Garlic and Parsley and Dry Fruit Cheese Balls

zzzzzzzzzzzzzzzzzzzzzzzzzzzzzzzzzzzzzzzzzzzzzzzzzzzz

22) Mini Cheese Balls

These mini cheese balls are very quick and easy to prepare. They are bite sized and so quickly eaten. They are particularly useful for kids and to give them in their lunch boxes. Below is its recipe:

Preparation time and serving: 1.5 hour and

Makes: 3

Ingredient List:

- Mozzarella cheese: 8 ounces
- Philadelphia cheese: 6 ounces
- Bacon strips: 1 pound
- Garlic powder: ½ tsp.
- Italian seasoning: ½ tsp.
- Chopped walnuts: for coating

zzzzzzzzzzzzzzzzzzzzzzzzzzzzzzzzzzzzzzzzzzzzzzzzzzzz

Instructions:

Take a bowl and mix the cream cheese and the mozzarella cheese. Mix properly and add the bacon strips, garlic powder and the Italian seasoning in cheese mixture. Mix everything properly and shape them into balls. Coat each ball properly with the chopped walnuts and place in the fridge for a few hours before serving them.

23) Cheesy Parsley Balls

This cheese ball recipe is a huge hit because the aromatic smell of the parsley along with its genuine taste literally sways a person's taste buds. Below is the recipe of it.

Total Prep Time: one hour

Makes: 10

Ingredient List:

- Mayonnaise: 1 Tbsp.
- Cream cheese: 8 ounces
- Lemon juice: 1 tsp.
- Shredded cheddar cheese: 1 cup
- Chopped onion: 1
- Chopped olives: ½ cup
- Dried parsley: ½ cup

zzzzzzzzzzzzzzzzzzzzzzzzzzzzzzzzzzzzzzzzzzzzzzzzzzzz

Instructions:

Take a bowl, and add in the cream cheese, mayonnaise, lemon juice, cheddar cheese and mix well. Now add in the chopped onion and chopped olives. Mix well until all ingredients are incorporated.

Make small balls from this mixture and put on a baking tray. Put this tray with cheese balls in the refrigerator for a few hours until they are set. Coat all balls in lots of dried parsley, or make a parsley dip. Serve chilled

24) Garlic Cheese Ball

Garlic is a favorite ingredient of many. It has a very nice taste and this recipe includes garlic as its core ingredient. You can even make a nice garlic dip to go with this cheese ball.

Total Prep Time: half hour

Makes: 10

Ingredient:

- Butter: ½ cup
- Cream cheese: 16 ounces
- Mustard: 1 Tbsp.
- Minced garlic: 1 Tbsp.
- Ranch dressing: ½ cup

zzzzzzzzzzzzzzzzzzzzzzzzzzzzzzzzzzzzzzzzzzzzzzzzzzzzz

Instructions:

In a bowl mix in the cream cheese and the melted butter. Now add the mustard and minced garlic. Stir in the ranch dressing in the end. Mix properly, form balls from the mixture and place them in the fridge to make them hard. Serve after few hours.

25) Lemon Cheese Balls

The citric taste of the lemons along with the salty flavor of the cheese will incorporate in to an amazing flavor. Check out the recipe of this lemon cheese balls.

Total Prep Time: half hour

Makes: 6

Ingredient List:

- Butter: ¼ cup
- Cream cheese: 8 ounces
- Sugar: ½ cup
- Lemonade mix: 1 Tbsp.
- Graham cracker crumbs: 1 cup

ZZZZZZZZZZZZZZZZZZZZZZZZZZZZZZZZZZZZZZZZZZZZZZZZZZZ

Instructions:

In this recipe you will need an electric mixer. In a bowl, beat butter, cream cheese, and sugar with your electric mixer. Add in the lemonade mix and blend all ingredients properly. Shape the mixture into balls. Refrigerate all balls for a few hours and coat the balls into graham cracker crumbs before serving.

26) Christmas Cheese Balls

This year you can try something new and exciting for your Christmas. Try out this new and latest recipe of the Christmas cheese balls.

Total Prep Time: 30 minutes

Serves: 20

Ingredient List:

- Cream cheese: 16 ounces
- Shredded cheddar cheese: 2 cups
- Onion chopped: ½
- Green bell pepper (chopped): 1
- Sliced Pimento peppers: as per taste
- Worcestershire sauce: 2 tsp.
- Salt: 1 pinch
- Lemon juice: 1 tsp.

zzzzzzzzzzzzzzzzzzzzzzzzzzzzzzzzzzzzzzzzzzzzzzzzzzzz

Instructions:

Mix the cream cheese and cheddar cheese in a bowl. Now add in the onion, green bell pepper, pimento pepper, Worcestershire sauce, salt and the lemon juice.

Mix all the ingredients together and form small balls with this mixture. Place them in a tray and keep in the fridge for a few hours before serving them.

27) Dried Fruit Cheese Ball

This is a very different and unusual cheese ball because it is coated with all kinds of dry fruits. Make sure you try it at your home.

Total Prep Time: half hour

Makes: 12

Ingredient List:

- Cream cheese: 8 ounces
- Honey: 2 Tbsp.
- Shredded cheddar cheese: 8 ounces
- Chopped pecans: 1 cup
- Dried fruits: 1 cup

zzzzzzzzzzzzzzzzzzzzzzzzzzzzzzzzzzzzzzzzzzzzzzzzzzzzzz

Instructions:

Mix cream cheese, honey, cheddar cheese and dried fruits in one. Make balls with this mixture and refrigerate all balls for a few hours.

Now roll balls in chopped pecans and again put them in the fridge to chill before serving.

About the Author

A native of Albuquerque, New Mexico, Sophia Freeman found her calling in the culinary arts when she enrolled at the Sante Fe School of Cooking. Freeman decided to take a year after graduation and travel around Europe, sampling the cuisine from small bistros and family owned restaurants from Italy to Portugal. Her bubbly personality and inquisitive nature made her popular with the locals in the villages and when she finished her trip and came home, she had made friends for life in the places she had visited. She also came home with a deeper understanding of European cuisine.

Freeman went to work at one of Albuquerque's 5-star restaurants as a sous-chef and soon worked her way up to head chef. The restaurant began to feature Freeman's original dishes as specials on the menu and soon after, she began to write e-books with her recipes. Sophia's dishes mix local flavours with European inspiration making them irresistible to the diners in her restaurant and the online community.

Freeman's experience in Europe didn't just teach her new ways of cooking, but also unique methods of presentation. Using rich sauces, crisp vegetables and meat cooked to perfection, she creates a stunning display as well as a delectable dish. She has won many local awards for her cuisine and she continues to delight her diners with her culinary masterpieces.

Author's Afterthoughts

I want to convey my big thanks to all of my readers who have taken the time to read my book. Readers like you make my work so rewarding and I cherish each and every one of you.

Grateful cannot describe how I feel when I know that someone has chosen my work over all of the choices available online. I hope you enjoyed the book as much as I enjoyed writing it.

Feedback from my readers is how I grow and learn as a chef and an author. Please take the time to let me know your thoughts by leaving a review on Amazon so I and your fellow readers can learn from your experience.

My deepest thanks,

Sophia Freeman

https://sophia.subscribemenow.com/

Made in the USA
Lexington, KY
21 July 2019